TRANSFORMING LEARNING AND DEVELOPMENT

The need for transformation

Do any of the following apply to you?

- Budgets for training are tight.
- Managers are finding it harder to release their staff for days at a time to attend training programmes.
- Travel budgets are under pressure making it harder for participants to travel to central training locations.
- Training providers are under greater pressure to demonstrate that their courses make a real difference.
- Face-to-face methods are not sufficiently scalable to train large numbers of people quickly.
- Learners are demanding more flexible ways to obtain the knowledge and skills that they need.
- You know you really have to make changes but you're not sure where to start.

If your answer to any of the above is 'yes' then it will be small comfort to know that you are not alone. The fact is that changes are necessary and sooner rather than later.

Over the past decade, as we in the learning and development profession have battled with almost unparalleled levels of uncertainty and pressure on resources, at The More Than Blended Company we have found ourselves engaged more and more often in discussions with learning providers, both external and in-house, looking to reinvent their offerings for their particular markets.

Of course this is not the first time that learning providers have had to struggle with tight market conditions. But this may well be the first time that customers – internal and external – are beginning to question the basis of the service offering. So what's changed?

First of all, customers cannot any longer afford for their employees to be off-job for protracted periods. That's because they don't have the spare capacity they once had to cover the time lost, and they need all hands on deck.

Some are also short on budget and, as we all know, training (particularly when external) is one of the easiest expenses to cut. However much we might protest that learning is an important investment for the future, I doubt if any company ever went bust because they delayed formal training when times were tight. We have to accept that fact and realise that learning is typically a medium to long term investment, and some organisations have not been so sure they have a medium to long term.

Customers are also more aware of the environmental impact of excessive employee travel. A good proportion of those cars on the motorway or planes in the air are carrying people to learning events, and not always in situations where face-to-face contact is essential to success. The environment may not be the biggest issue on anyone's agenda right now, but it will return as economic conditions improve. By then, many organisations will have got used to the idea that many meetings and other events can be handled perfectly adequately using web conferencing.

Finally, there is an increasing awareness that stand-alone classroom interventions have a limited impact on job performance. However enjoyable they may be at the time, and however high the knowledge assessment scores might be at the end, these are no guarantee that what is learned will be retained, applied and then put to good use.

In this short publication, we'll start by developing a vision for a transformed learning and development function; one that is aligned, economical, scalable, flexible, engaging and, above all, powerful in terms of the results it achieves. We'll move on to look at some of the changes that can be made to realise this vision, expressed as six shifts:

- from generic to tailored solutions
- from synchronous to asynchronous
- from compliance to competence
- from top-down to bottom-up
- from courses to resources
- from face-to-face to online

In each case we'll be making clear that these are shifts along a continuum, not the abandonment of practices that clearly deliver results. We'll also keep reminding you that every situation is different and that every organisation needs to strike its own balance.

Lastly, we'll spell out a process that will get you started on the journey to transformation, starting with a thorough analysis of your particular requirements, target populations and constraints. We'll look at the implications these have in terms of your learning architecture and infrastructure, the way you analyse performance needs and design blended solutions, and the skills you'll need if you are to take advantage of new learning technologies.

A VISION FOR TRANSFORMATION

We start by developing a vision for a transformed learning and development function; one that is aligned, economical, scalable, flexible, engaging and, above all, powerful in terms of the results it achieves.

Aligned

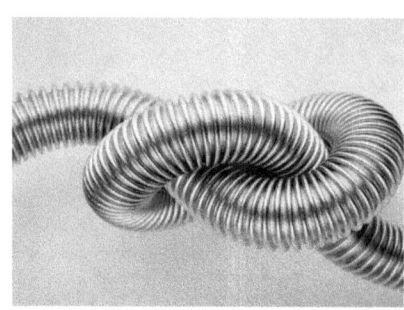

Flexible

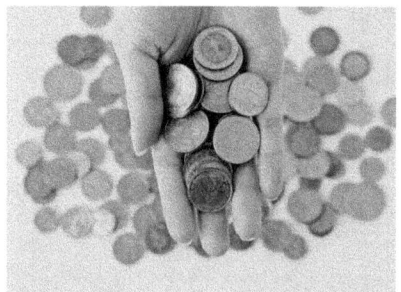

Economical

Engaging

Scalable

Powerful

Learning and development that is aligned

It is nothing new to be told that training should be aligned to the needs of the business, but that doesn't mean that it 'goes without saying' or is 'common sense'. All too often, common sense is anything but common.

Ask yourself how many of the training interventions in your organisation are clearly aligned to current business needs, rather than fulfilling requirements articulated sometime in the distant past, but with no current relevance. And how many interventions have originated from the l&d department on the basis of where they believe the organisation should be heading, regardless of the views of senior management?

No organisation ever set up an l&d department for them to then determine the direction for the organisation. It is not up to learning professionals to decide what is good leadership, what is good customer service or what are appropriate values for the organisation. Their job is to help senior management make their vision a reality, regardless of whether that vision is shared by the professionals that staff the l&d department.

A good question to ask is this:

What behaviours are critical to the future success of this organisation?

Let's unpick this a little. You need to know about 'behaviours' because, of all the various factors which influence the success of an organisation, only these can be influenced by learning and development. You need to find out which are the 'critical' behaviours, because you don't have the resources to devote to the non-critical. And you need to focus on 'future success', because learning and development is an investment in the future and can do little to influence what happens right now. The only people who can answer this question with any authority are senior management.

The question can and should also be addressed for each of the main functional and regional departments and divisions within the organisation, as well as at various levels. For example: 'What behaviours are critical to the future success of the IT department or European region'; 'What middle management behaviours are critical to the future success of the organisation?'

Once you know what behaviours are required if the organisation is to succeed in the future, you need to assess the extent of the task in front of you:

To what degree are employees already exhibiting the behaviours that are critical for success?

Answering this question is no small task. If you work for a larger organisation, then ideally you'll have set up a performance management system that enables you to keep track of how individuals are performing. This will include a competency framework covering every job position; one that is up-to-date with the constant and inevitable changes in job responsibilities and which describes the behaviours that senior management are looking to encourage. In order for you to assess the extent to which these competences are evidenced in actual performance, all employees will have been regularly assessed against this framework or will have conducted some form of self-assessment. Smaller organisations may not have gone so far, but they should at very least be conducting regular performance appraisals.

If, having carried out your research, you find no gaps, then your only problem is ensuring the continued supply of employees who exhibit the desired behaviours. You should be so lucky! Chances are you'll have to ask one more question:

What influence can learning and development have on these behaviours?

Performance is influenced by a lot more than skill and knowledge. Situational influences on the performer include the clarity of roles and objectives, the suitability of the working environment, and the tools and other resources at the performer's disposal.

The performer him or herself has aptitudes (indicating his or her potential to learn) and motivations, as well as their accumulated knowledge and skills. The performer's responses are also influenced by outcomes (the incentives and disincentives that are likely to result from performing in a certain way) as well as the timely availability of relevant feedback.

The whole performance system has to be functioning correctly if performers are to exhibit the desired behaviours. Learning and development is only going to work if (1) variability in performance can at least partly be attributed to a lack of knowledge or skills, and (2) the employees in question have the aptitude to acquire them.

Learning professionals may have to be assertive in conducting and communicating this sort of logical analysis. As Wick, Pollock, Jefferson and Flanagan remind us, 'The problem typically begins when someone in upper management decrees that the company needs to have a programme on some particular topic. And when the goal of having a programme is defined as "having a programme", the initiative is in trouble from the start.'

Senior managers may be experts in determining the problems that are getting in the way of performance, but they are not experts in finding the solutions – that's your job, and this is your time to speak up.

Learning and development that is economical

It almost goes without saying in today's testing times that learning and development needs to be economical. In fact, there has always been this need. It is incumbent on any manager, regardless of function, to utilise as few of the organisation's resources as possible in fulfilling their responsibilities. L&d is no different. It makes no difference whether you regard training as a cost or an investment. If a cost, then the organisation's profits will be maximised by keeping this to a minimum. If an investment, then you are obligated to keep this as small as it can be without unduly threatening the returns.

Although it is dangerous to generalise, it is probably fair to say that, until 2008 and the credit crunch, l&d budgets had not been the subject of much critical examination as long as they were in line with historical levels and comparable to those of other, similar organisations. This situation changed and how. Budgets in the USA took a hit of 20% or more and the story in Europe was not so different.

Even richer organisations, not seemingly under pressure, became defensive about expenditure. Conserving cash was the name of the game. Senior managers no longer took the l&d budget as a given; it had to be justified from the bottom-up as just one of a number of means for influencing performance and competitiveness. This should always have been the case. It is best to assume that, from now on, it always will be.

One way that l&d can have a much greater influence on organisational expenditure is by making sure that it considers the full cost of any intervention, not just the obvious expenditure which requires a cheque to be written.

By far the greatest cost in any intervention is learner time. Every hour spent away from productive work is a cost to the organisation and one that should be minimised. Sometimes this cost is directly visible because overtime has to be paid or contractors brought in to cover the lost time. But even if this is not the case, the cost is still real; time spent learning could have been used productively elsewhere – in other words, there is an opportunity cost.

Indirect costs occur within the l&d department as well. Time spent by salaried staff on design, development and delivery of any intervention should be costed against that intervention. And yes, we are proposing that time sheets are maintained, so the cost can be accurately monitored.

It is hard to argue against accurate budgeting and cost monitoring of l&d interventions, yet this is very rarely carried out in practice. Yes, the obvious, direct, external costs – like the use of external trainers and digital content developers – are closely watched, but these are only a small proportion of the true cost.

It's time l&d took responsibility for its true effect on the finances of the organisations that it serves.

Learning and development that is scalable

Learning interventions are scalable when they are capable of delivering high quality results to ever-larger audiences.

There's little doubt that, when used for the right purpose and well executed, one-to-one learning can be extremely effective, but it is hardly scalable; after all, there are only so many hours in a day that any instructor, coach or mentor can dedicate to the task. While there is often a need to include an element of one-to-one or small group learning in a blend, because that's the only way of making sure the job gets done properly, there are many occasions on which far more scalable methods can be applied.

Some fantastic progress has been made in the past five years in realising the concept of massively scalable education. Particularly exciting examples are the Khan Academy, which has contributed to the maths education of hundreds of millions, and the MOOCS (large-scale free online courses) being run by major universities and many others. One of the first, An Introduction to Artificial Intelligence, led by Peter Norvig and Sebastian Thrun, attracted more than one hundred thousand registrations, of which tens of thousands made it through to its conclusion. If you are not familiar with these projects, you can see Khan, Norvig and Thrun discussing the implications of their work in Reinventing Education - 45 minutes of very watchable YouTube video.

So, yes, you can teach maths and science to millions at practically no cost using videos and quizzes, and this is a fantastic step forward, but can we make similar gains in workplace learning? Currently, skills development is a labour-intensive and very costly business, typically involving a great deal of face-to-face contact with a trainer or coach. Some individuals, some organisations, and some countries have been able to afford this and will be able to sustain this investment even in a harsh economic climate. That leaves an awful lot of skills gaps and unemployed people.

The pressure for more scalable learning and development at work is accentuated by the increased pace at which change takes place within organisations. More often than not there simply isn't the time available to wait for 'high-touch' training. L&d needs a plan B; one that much better leverages limited subject expertise and teaching skills.

Learning and development that is flexible

Flexibility is an important element in the vision for a transformed l&d. What it implies is more control for l&d's ultimate customers – the employees of an organisation. Adults expect to have control over what they learn, when and where, and they will increasingly demand it. They expect flexibility because they have grown accustomed to finding whatever information they need at the click of a mouse from Google, YouTube and Wikipedia.

Synchronous learning (that takes place with others, at a specific time, typically in a physical or virtual classroom) can be powerful, but it is certainly not flexible. It means you have to compromise on *when* you learn in order to suit others. Similarly, face-to-face learning can add a great deal of value when used for the right purposes, but is highly inflexible. Being face-to-face means you have to compromise on *where* you learn in order to suit others.

Flexibility can take many forms. For the learner it can mean:

Controlling what you learn and to what level: So much traditional training is one-size-fits-all: everybody starts and ends at the same place, regardless of need. But every learner is different in terms of their prior knowledge and goals, and it is not rocket science to organise training in a modular fashion. Providing this sort of flexibility is not always practical, but it should at least be an aim.

Controlling how you learn: This is a tricky one, because there has been a lot of nonsense talked about learning styles and how different we are in how we like to learn, yet we are actually much more alike than we are different and it is usually uneconomical to offer training in alternative forms. However, there are sometimes obstacles that get in the way of learners taking advantage of a particular form of learning (disabilities, access to technology, inability to travel, etc.) and providing alternatives can be beneficial, if not always practical.

Controlling when you learn and at what pace: By and large, learners would prefer not to have to wait to learn something that is important to their work. They'd also like to control when they learn, for how long, how fast and how slow. Having to conform to someone else's timetable is always going to be a compromise solution.

Controlling where you learn: Having to travel to a central location for training is sometimes necessary, but is typically an expensive and time-consuming activity – if you can avoid it you should. It also makes sense to provide learners with the opportunity to continue their learning when they are on the move, so they can take advantage of the inevitable dead times on trains, in airports and hotel rooms.

Of course it can be extremely difficult to provide all this flexibility without impacting heavily on our other objectives of scalability and economy – we have to strike the right balance. But flexibility is a worthwhile target to have in mind and you can make big strides in this direction by creating more modular interventions, with a greater use of self-paced components, and by delivering online when possible.

Learning and development that is engaging

Learning interventions need to be engaging, because without learner engagement there's very little chance that any meaningful learning will take place. Engaging interventions attract and maintain interest, they arouse the emotions, they are full of energy. Just like learning should be.

In *Switch – How to Change Things When Change is Hard*, by Chip and Dan Heath, the authors make a key distinction between what we think consciously and what our more primitive, emotional system will have us do. They liken the emotional system to an elephant and the intellect to the rider of the elephant. As you can imagine, when you're trying hard to resist that bar of chocolate or force yourself up out of bed on a cold morning, the rider has a heck of a job keeping the elephant under control and can easily become exhausted in the process.

Engaging the learner is about getting the elephant on board. While the rider may be engaged by the long-term benefits of a learning activity or by pure intellectual curiosity, the elephant is much more interested in what's in it for him right now.

The prospect of a solution to a real, current problem will definitely do the job, because relevance will always drive out resistance. The elephant may also be motivated by a challenge – perhaps a game which involves some form of competition. Humour may also do the trick, as will plain novelty.

Being engaged can be likened to a state of 'flow', as described by the psychologist Mihaly Csiksczentmihalyi. He explains this state as follows:

- Confronting tasks that we have a chance of completing

- Concentration

- Clear goals

- Immediate feedback

- A deep, effortless involvement

- A sense of control over one's actions

- A reduced concern for self

- Hours passing by in minutes

You may find it a daunting challenge to design and deliver learning interventions that are capable of inducing such a state of mind, but in the right circumstances the motivation to learn can be very strong.

As Daniel Pink describes in **Drive: The Surprising Truth About What Motivates Us**, three factors stand out: the desire to direct our own lives; the urge to get better and better at something that matters; and the yearning to do what we do in the service of something larger than ourselves. Provide learning opportunities with a clear purpose, a direct relevance to real-world issues and a highly-flexible and learner-centred methodology and you'll be more than half the way there.

Learning and development that is powerful

Clearly, learning interventions are of little or no value to an organisation if they don't have a positive impact on key performance indicators. There is a clear link here with alignment. For learning interventions to be powerful, they have first to be aligned to the organisation's current and future needs.

Employers are not, of course, the only stakeholders in workplace learning, even if they pay the bill. Learning is first and foremost an investment in the learner, the employee. It can also be regarded as an investment by learners themselves, who must be engaged if learning is to take place at all. A learning activity is powerful for a learner if it helps them to achieve mastery in their particular area of work and to build their confidence so that they find work more fulfilling and enjoyable.

So, what causes one learning intervention to be more powerful than another? Well, we have already established that the process has to start with alignment to the organisation's and the learners' requirements, neither of which will happen by magic or guesswork. The only way to assess requirements is to consult with all the relevant stakeholders and that's a time-consuming process.

An intervention also needs to teach the right things. This might seem obvious, but it is perfectly possible for an intervention to do a very effective job of developing the wrong knowledge and skills.

For example, let's say an organisation wants to increase turnover by adopting a new sales process. They could run a wonderful course which transfers efficiently back to the job. But if the new sales process itself is flawed, then the net result may be lower sales not higher.

Thirdly, the intervention needs to be designed and delivered effectively. The research tells us that effective learning is largely down to choosing the right strategies and methods, and then implementing them well. Media choices, such as whether a particular activity or resource is delivered face-to-face or online, are certainly going to have an impact on flexibility, cost and time-efficiency, but will not usually determine whether or not the learning outcomes are achieved (if you doubt this, check online for Thomas L Russell's **The No Significant Difference Phenomenon**).

Lastly, the power of an intervention will very often depend on the commitment of learners' managers. Newstrom and Broad found that the positive involvement of managers before and after an intervention was more likely to influence the end result than any actions by trainers and by learners themselves.

2

STRATEGIES FOR TRANSFORMATION

We move on to look at six ways in which learning professionals can realise a transformation in the way that learning and development occurs in their organisations. These strategies make it possible to satisfy all six elements in the vision for change, i.e. learning that is aligned, economical, scalable, flexible, engaging and powerful.

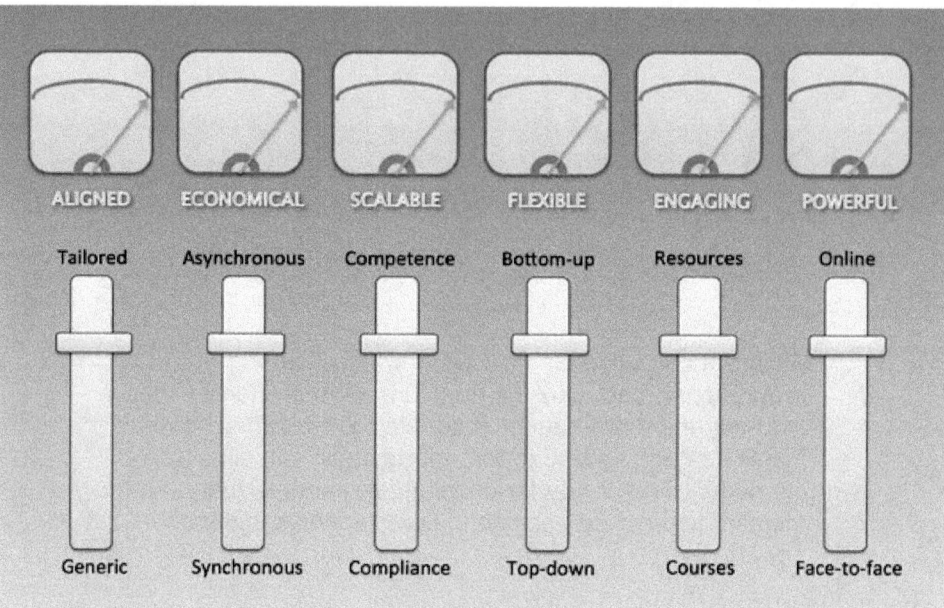

From generic to tailored

The first step on the route to transformation is a shift from interventions that are generic to those that are more tailored. Like each of the recommendations that follow, this change represents a movement of a slider, not a switch on or off. Every organisation is different: some may already offer highly tailored solutions, others will have good reasons for sticking with a more generic approach. However, a great deal of current l&d offerings can be categorised as 'one size fits no-one', a sheep dip approach in which everyone receives the same learning experience, regardless of their prior knowledge and need.

It might seem counter-productive when resources are very tight to offer a more personalised service, but there are ways in which this can be achieved economically:

- You can start by adopting a more modular architecture for your interventions. This allows employees to pick and choose from the ingredients they need to make their own perfectly balanced meal. Modularity implies a more granular structure – activities and resources must be provided in much smaller chunks. Modular structures are not only more flexible, they also provide improved results because they are less likely to overload learners.

- To help employees to make more informed decisions about their requirements (and to reassure employers that important needs are not going un-met) make available diagnostic tools which pre-assess knowledge and (if possible) skills.

- Don't shy away from one-to-one support where it's needed. While it is increasingly uneconomic to provide whole solutions on a one-to-one basis, discriminating use of tutor support, access to experts and coaching can make all the difference. If just 5% of a solution is offered in this way (and some learners won't use it at all, some a lot more) then your interventions are much more likely to make a real difference.

- If you're a little more ambitious, build online content that intelligently adapts to the learner's progress.

The benefits

So what effect does pushing the slider from generic to tailored have on the six elements of our transformation vision?

- **Aligned:** Almost by definition, a tailored solution is going to be better aligned to requirements than a generic one, just as a bespoke suit will fit better than one bought off-the-shelf.

- **Economical:** Frankly, this move is unlikely to make your offerings more economical. You may gain from less courses being taken that are not really needed, but you'll lose by adding one-to-one support.

- **Scalable:** Again, it's hard to argue that tailored interventions are more scalable, so we'll have to gain scalability through other actions.

- **Flexible:** We've already seen that tailored offerings are more flexible, because the learner gets more choice to configure a solution that works for them.

- **Engaging:** One of the most important elements (if not the most important) in engagement is relevance and relevance drives out resistance. When you get to choose the elements which are best suited to your needs then you can cut out days spent trying to keep awake on unnecessary classroom events and endless clicking through meaningless pages of e-learning.

- **Powerful:** You would expect tailored interventions to be more powerful because they are aimed at real needs and respond to individual differences. And, in the end, powerful learning is what it's all about.

From synchronous to asynchronous

The second step on the route to transformation is a shift from interventions that are synchronous to those that are asynchronous. In case you're not familiar with the jargon, 'synchronous' learning activities happen in real-time – they are 'live'. The most obvious examples are classroom courses and on-the-job training sessions, but within this category we can also include the use of the telephone and live online tools, such as instant messaging, Skype and virtual classrooms. The defining characteristic of a synchronous activity is that all the participants have to be available at the same time.

'Asynchronous' activities, on the other hand, are self-paced; they allow the learner to determine when and for how long they undertake self-study activities or communicate with fellow learners or trainers. Reading a book, watching a video, listening to a podcast, surfing the web or interacting with an e-learning programme are all asynchronous; so is communicating by post, by text messages, by email or through forums, blogs, wikis and social networks.

Like each of the recommendations in this section, the change from synchronous to asynchronous represents a movement of a slider, not a switch on or off. Every organisation is different and needs to find its own balance.

The argument for being synchronous

There is nothing inherently wrong with synchronous communication. It gets things done quickly. It allows a learner to get speedy answers to questions and to obtain quick feedback on their performance. It makes it possible for learners to work together on practical activities such as role-plays. It allows for free-flowing discussions and is altogether more relaxed and sociable.

Synchronous events also act as milestones in a blended solution. Because they are scheduled to happen at a particular date and time, they get blocked out in the diary and are less likely to be put off to another day. They also act as a convenient deadline for activities that are self-paced.

All in all then, it's usually a good thing for a proportion of a learning solution to be synchronous.

So, if it ain't broke, why try and fix it?

Although synchronous learning events, such as classroom courses, have their benefits, they also come with snags:

- Having to organise dates and times that suit everyone is tiresome and time-consuming. In some situations, in which learners are based in different time zones or have all sorts of existing commitments, it can sometimes prove impossible.

- Waiting for a date and time can hold you up from learning what you want to do right now.

- Synchronous events can be more stressful, because you will often be put under pressure to make quick responses to questions and discussion topics. You also have no control over the pace at which you learn, which is a particular problem if you start with less prior knowledge than your colleagues.

- An important element of learning is reflection and that's not easy to accomplish when you're under time pressure.

- Every learner is different in terms of their needs, prior knowledge and preferences. Live events are simply not flexible enough to cope with all these differences.

The benefits

So what effect does pushing the slider from synchronous to asynchronous have on the six elements of our transformation vision?

- **Aligned:** There's no real change here, because synchronous and asynchronous activities can be equally well-aligned.

- **Economical:** There could be some benefits here, particularly in terms of the amount of time consumed by the learning activity. Generally self-paced learning is quicker, as much as anything because learners can access the material they want and ignore what is less relevant. There's also the possibility that learners can get faster to competence, because they are not having to wait about before receiving the training they need.

- **Scalable:** Here's a real plus, because many more people can be learning at the same time.

- **Flexible:** This is an obvious one. The main purpose of increasing the asynchronous component is to improve flexibility.

- **Engaging:** You might lose something here, because live events will, for most people, be more urgent and engaging.

- **Powerful:** Asynchronous activities are not inherently more powerful, but having a better balance between synchronous and asynchronous elements is likely to show performance benefits, if for no other reason than that learners have more time to reflect.

From compliance to competence

The third step on the route to transformation is a shift from interventions aimed primarily at ensuring compliance to those that aim to achieve competency.

Now every organisation does, to some extent, have to comply with regulations of one sort or another, whether that relates to employment policies, health and safety, the prevention of money laundering, the marketing of pharmaceutical products, and so on.

The implications of breaking these regulations – and being found out – can be devastating for an organisation, not only financially, but in terms of public reputation. In extreme cases, executives and others lower down in an organisation can face criminal charges. It is not surprising, then, that organisations – sometimes on the insistence of their insurers – take great pains to ensure that infringements are kept to a minimum. An obvious step in achieving this is to ensure everyone involved obtains adequate training.

There are two ways of looking at this sort of training:

- you can regard it as a simple box-ticking exercise in which employers and employees go through the motions of delivering and receiving training, in order to satisfy regulators and insurers that the job is being done; or

- you aim to bring about a shift in behaviour such that infringements are very unlikely to occur, because employees believe in the policy and have the necessary knowledge and skill to put it into practice.

The first option is based on the assumptions that infringements are unlikely, the regulations are a nuisance and that compliance is a necessary evil. The second option is founded on the principles that infringements can and do happen, that the regulations are rightly in place to prevent harm to third parties, and that policies are not enough – delivering on these policies requires competence. Quite a difference.

The implications of an approach based on compliance

So what are the dangers of basing your approach to training on simple compliance?

- Executives and learning professionals regard the whole exercise as a box-ticking exercise.

- The training is designed to deliver as much dry and abstract information as possible in the minimum time. Subject-matter experts rather than learning professionals drive the design.

- Knowledge is typically assessed immediately after delivery of the information, invalidating the results. No effort is made to assess whether this information can be applied effectively in context, in other words whether the training has resulted in behaviour change.

- Employees will do the minimum possible to complete the training, focusing all their attention on passing the assessment rather than on gaining useful information that is important for their job.

- On the basis that people resist 'being changed', it is possible that the whole process makes them less likely to comply rather than more so.

- E-learning is often used as the means of delivery in order to minimise costs and take the pressure off trainers who understandably don't want to deliver training that nobody wants. As a result, e-learning becomes synonymous with compliance and bad training generally.

Shifting the emphasis to competence

How would the picture change if a genuine attempt were made to ensure competence?

- Executives and learning professionals would themselves be committed to change and would model the desired behaviour consistently.

- The training would focus on encouraging positive attitudes to the necessary change, providing critically-important information (the rest can be accessed as reference resources), putting principles into context with examples and case studies and, most importantly, providing plenty of opportunities for practice (with supportive feedback).

- Employees are assessed on the basis of their ability to apply what they have learned in context rather than their ability to retain information.

- Management reinforces the desired behaviour when it is put into practice.

- E-learning is used when it is an appropriate medium for delivering particular elements of what is likely to be a blended solution.

The benefits

So what effect does pushing the slider from compliance to competence have on the six elements of our transformation vision?

- **Aligned:** Courses oriented to building competence can be directly aligned to business needs. This means genuinely complying with the requirements of regulators, not just going through the motions of delivering compliance training.

- **Economical:** Sorry, but competence-based training will cost more to deliver. On the other hand, have you factored in the real risk of a billion dollar lawsuit?

- **Scalable:** Again, quality comes at a cost. Simple self-study courses may be cheaper, but are they really achieving a positive return?

- **Flexible:** To be honest there's not going to be a lot of change here. If anything, more elaborate blends are going to be less easy to complete than those that concentrate on ticking the boxes. So, no more asking your assistant to click through the screens on your behalf.

- **Engaging:** As we've seen already, relevance drives out resistance. Who's going to be engaged by a box-ticking exercise?

- **Powerful:** And here's the bottom line. Competency-based training really will protect you from risk and surely that's the whole point.

From top-down to bottom-up

The fourth step on the route to transformation is a shift from learning and development activities that are directed from the top-down to those that originate from the bottom-up.

Top-down learning

Top-down learning occurs because organisations want their employees to perform effectively and efficiently and they appreciate that this depends, at least in part, on employees possessing the appropriate knowledge and skills. Top-down learning is designed to fulfil the employer's objectives, not the employees'.

Whatever the attractions of a more bottom-up approach (as we shall see), some learning cannot be left to chance. Why? Because employees need basic competencies and they don't always know what they don't know, where to look for answers or who to turn to; also because requirements change (new policies, products, plans) and because employees must be developed to fill future gaps.

However, it is unrealistic for all learning to be managed on a top-down basis, particularly in those organisations where change is constant and knowledge requirements hard to predict. As most top-down learning requires the direct intervention of subject experts and learning professionals, resources are clearly going to be limited and so priorities have to be determined.

Top-down learning is likely to be most valuable for the 20% of knowledge that is needed 80% of the time, and for learning that is most critical in terms of risk to safety, finances or reputation.

Bottom-up learning

Bottom-up learning occurs because employees also want to perform. The exact motivation may vary, from achieving job security to earning more money, gaining recognition or obtaining personal fulfilment, but the route to all these is performing well on the job, and employees know as well as their employers that this depends – again, at least in part – on them acquiring the appropriate knowledge and skills.

Bottom-up learning is managed by employees themselves. It addresses the 80% of knowledge that is needed 20% of the time and is particularly important in those organisations in which there is constant change and fluidity in tasks and goals.

Bottom-up learning is cheaper, more responsive, less controlling, less patronising and altogether more in tune with the times. But it is also less certain, less measurable and less suited to dependent learners who don't know what they don't know.

For bottom-up learning to thrive, employees need the motive, the means and the opportunity (just like the perpetrators in crime novels). They will only have the **motive** if they are rewarded for effective performance. They will only have the **means** if employers help them to develop the skills they need to learn independently and provide, where appropriate, the right collaborative software tools (a rich and searchable intranet, forums, wikis, blogs, communities of practice, etc.). They will only have the **opportunity** if employers are able to foster a culture which encourages self-initiative and does not overly penalise mistakes.

Learning professionals could do worse in future than to regard bottom-up learning as the default solution, the one on which they rely except when it is obviously unsuitable. For too long, employees have been spoon-fed their education and their training, and have failed to develop as independent learners to the extent that perhaps they should have done. Those now entering the workforce have, in many cases, overcome these barriers and have higher expectations. Provide them with the motive, the means and the opportunities and their capabilities are likely to astound you.

The benefits

So what effect does pushing the slider from top-down to bottom-up have on the six elements of our transformation vision?

- **Aligned:** This particular change should not have a major impact on alignment.

- **Economical:** Some investment might need to be made in collaborative tools, but otherwise bottom-up learning requires little or no additional expense.

- **Scalable:** Bottom-up learning is highly scalable because it draws upon the expertise of every employee. In a bottom-up learning culture, everyone is a teacher and everyone a learner; no-one knows everything and everyone knows something.

- **Flexible:** Here is the greatest advantage. Bottom-up learning occurs as and when it is needed; it responds organically to changes in requirements.

- **Engaging:** There's not likely to be much impact here, except perhaps to the extent that bottom-up learning is likely to be more relevant to current needs.

- **Powerful:** It could be argued that bottom-up learning will be less powerful because it is not so professionally conceived and delivered, but this factor could easily be over-weighed by greater relevance and increased responsiveness.

From courses to resources

The fifth step on the route to transformation is a shift from courses to resources. We've borrowed this terminology from Nick Shackleton-Jones. Nick distinguishes between the formal nature of courses (where the focus, he believes, should be on engaging learners emotionally with the topic and on building their confidence to continue to learn independently) and the on-going provision of resources, both human and in the form of content, to support employees as they continue to learn and apply their new skills.

Why courses are not enough

Courses have, historically, been what l&d does, perhaps even its raison d'être; and they will continue to play an important role, particularly with novices who 'don't know what they don't know' and when formal confirmation is required that particular learning objectives have been achieved.

Courses may take place in a classroom, online, on-job or by some blend of these, but they all typically have objectives, entry criteria, a curriculum, formal content, tuition and assessment. More often than not they also take place at a predetermined time and are 'pushed' at a particular population. All of this structure helps an organisation to make sure that certain key interventions do take place in the intended fashion but does not guarantee success. All too often, courses fail to fulfil their aims:

- They are frequently forced on those who don't need them.

- Timing is rarely ideal – often they are too early or too late.

- They are frequently knowledge-focused and, as a result, serve only to overwhelm the learner with new information, without placing this in context.

- They typically provide nowhere near enough opportunity for practice and feedback.

- They make little provision for follow-up once the course has been completed.

The case for resources

There's nothing wrong with courses as such, it's just that we place too much attention on them and not enough on what happens afterwards. By and large, we would do well to teach much less and provide much more in the way of support. Courses are for stories, scenarios, simulations and discussions; resources are where you go to find the information you need to follow up on your interest.

These resources can take many forms:

- Experts that we can call upon for information.

- Coaches who can help us to analyse our successes and failures and establish our goals.

- Packaged content that can provide us with information and help in diagnosing problems and making decisions.

- Forums and other collaborative tools that allow us to share expertise and solve problems.

The argument for shifting the emphasis from teaching everything formally up-front to teaching the essentials and then providing other information on-demand has strengthened over the past few years:

- We now have a much better understanding of how easy it is to overwhelm novices with information and how little of this information is retained.

- The easy availability of information through search engines and on mobile devices makes it much more practical to provide resources as and when needed.

- Expectations have changed. Employees no longer assume they will have to learn large quantities of information up-front, when it can so easily be made available on-demand.

The benefits

So what effect does pushing the slider from courses to resources have on the six elements of our transformation vision?

- **Aligned:** There is nothing about the move from courses to resources that will make an impact here.

- **Economical:** In this respect you should see an improvement, because resources are much more economical to provide than courses.

- **Scalable:** Courses take a lot of time and effort to manage. Resources can be made available to large audiences with little difficulty.

- **Flexible:** Because resources are available on demand, the learner is in complete control over what they access and when.

- **Engaging:** Slimmed-down courses that focus on must-know information and key skills, and which provide plenty of opportunities for practice will be much more engaging. With resources, engagement is not the issue – you only call upon a resource when you need it.

- **Powerful:** Most importantly, the courses and resources combination gets the job done in terms of improved competency on-the-job.

From face-to-face to online

The sixth and last step on the route to transformation is a shift from delivering learning face-to-face to delivering online. There are obvious benefits from learning online in terms of flexibility, as well as savings in terms of time, budget and carbon emissions, but old habits die hard and many learning professionals are finding it hard to make the change.

Of course, not all learning can be brought online while maintaining quality, for example:

• Some interpersonal skills courses require tutors and/or participants to be able to accurately monitor the body language of others.

• Some practical courses require students to interact with equipment in ways that cannot feasibly be simulated online.

• Some courses benefit from the opportunities provided for networking socially.

• Some skills are more authentically practised in the real job environment.

But, as a whole, we tend to exaggerate the extent to which our face-to-face events really need to remain that way. It is worth reflecting on how we consume media in our personal lives. Of the music we listen to, only a small proportion is in a club or concert hall. Of the drama we consume, most is on the TV or in the cinema, not the theatre. Of the sport we watch, the overwhelming majority is on TV. When we do go to a theatre, concert hall or sports stadium, it is a very special event, often one we will remember for a very long time. But for most of us, this is not normal practice.

The benefits

So what effect does pushing the slider from face-to-face to online have on the six elements of our transformation vision?

- **Aligned:** No real impact in this case.

- **Economical:** There are obvious benefits here, as time and money is saved by removing the need for travel. Learning time also tends to be reduced, because there is less of a temptation for course designers to fill a whole day or week with training when the time is not strictly needed.

- **Scalable:** Face-to-face events are constrained in terms of scalability because of the practical limitation of space. Eighty thousand people may have been able to watch the 100m final at the Olympics in London, but hundreds of millions could watch remotely, not only on TV but online. As the providers of MOOCs (massively open online courses) have discovered, while a lecture room might be packed to capacity with 200 students, a thousand times more could take part in an online lecture.

- **Flexible:** Online learning is, above all, more flexible because it frees the learner from the constraints of geography. An online learner can access what learning they want, wherever they want, without the time, financial and environmental costs of travel.

- **Engaging:** There is no reason why an online experience should necessarily be less engaging than one which is face-to-face, assuming it is relevant and well-designed, but there is still a certain magic about 'being there,' particularly when the opportunities are scarce, e.g. the big game, the farewell tour, the invited audience. You will never quite be able to match this experience in a live online event, but whether this really matters in a learning and development context is debatable.

- **Powerful:** There is no reason why there should be an impact here.

In summary

If you push the faders on all six strategies, you can maximise every element of your vision, as you can see from the 'mixer' on the next page. While some of the strategies have positive and negative consequences, when used in combination the pluses greatly outweigh the minuses and allow you to achieve all your goals.

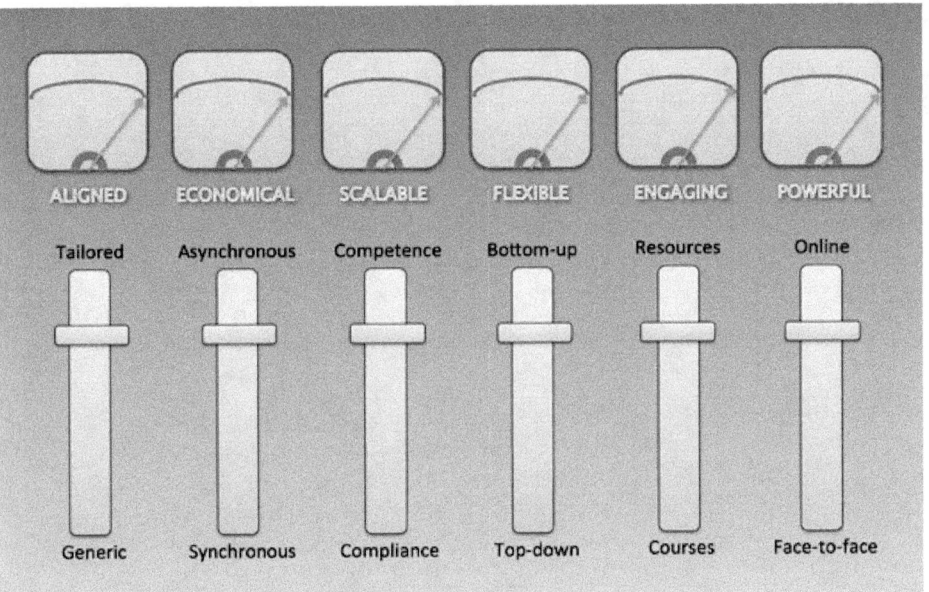

3

MAKING TRANSFORMATION HAPPEN

In this last section, we focus on the practical steps we can take to make transformation happen:

- Recognising the uniqueness of your particular organisation in terms of its requirements, the characteristics of its people and the constraints that govern its decision-making.

- Establishing a learning architecture and infrastructure that recognises these unique characteristics.

- Putting in place processes for improved performance needs analysis and blended solution design.

- Building capability in areas such as the design of digital learning content, learning live and online, and connected online learning.

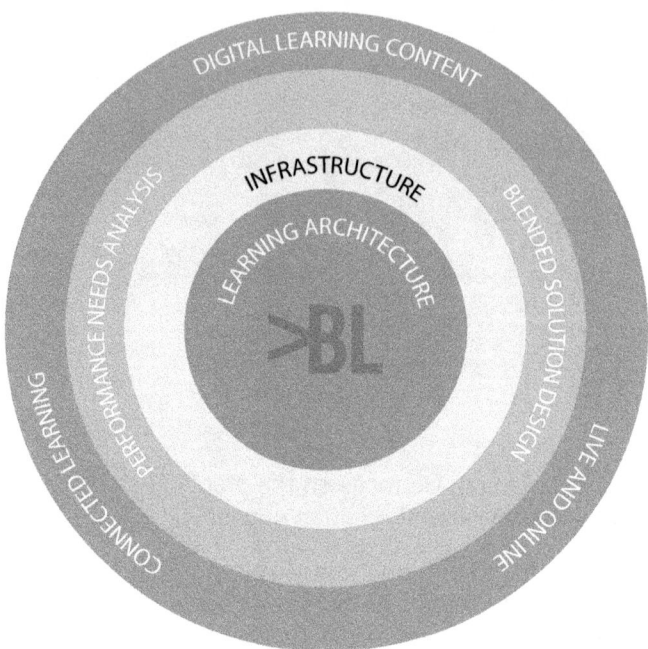

How organisations differ

So far, we have set out a vision and strategies for transformation in workplace learning and development as they would apply to some generic organisation. Needless to say, that organisation only exists in abstract. If you've got this far, then hopefully you'll have bought into some of the ideas, but you'll also probably have encountered recommendations that make little or no sense for the environment in which you work. Clearly every organisation needs its own vision and strategy for transformation, shaped around its own unique characteristics.

So what are the characteristics that make the most difference? In our experience, they can be summarised under three headings: the requirements in terms of learning, the characteristics of the employee population, and the particular opportunities and constraints that shape decision-making. We call these 'the three Ls' – learning, learners and logistics.

Learning

Each organisation (and each department, division and horizontal slice within this) has particular requirements for learning. Strictly speaking these requirements are actually for improved performance because, unless the organisation is a school or college, it is only indirectly measured in terms of the learning it manages to bring about.

And if, as learning professionals, we focus our efforts on improving performance, then we have to take a broad view of what 'learning' actually encompasses. Increasingly it is not just the knowledge, skills and attitudes required to support performance, but access to just-in-time information.

Strictly speaking, information cannot be regarded as learning, because it just needs to be applied rather than memorised, but that does not diminish its importance in our overall strategy for transformation.

An organisation's requirements for learning (and just-in-time information) should be directly aligned to its goals and strategy (you will remember that alignment is one of the six key elements in our vision for a transformed l&d). An organisation's requirements are likely to be many and varied, but one or more of the following types of learning is likely to be of particular importance:

- Understanding and committing to the organisation's mission, values, policies and strategies.

- Understanding the organisation's work processes.

- Keeping up-to-date with inevitable changes and developments in what we need to know and be able to do.

- Performing routine administrative tasks.

- Solving problems and making judgements.

- Communicating using electronic media.

- Interacting person-to-person with peers, direct reports, customers, suppliers and other third parties.

- Interacting with the physical world, with vehicles and with equipment.

You will undoubtedly think of more examples. These distinctions matter because each type of learning demands a different approach in terms of delivery. Each addresses a different form of knowledge, skill or attitude and impacts, therefore, on the extent to which you will want to make the six strategic shifts described previously.

For example, in one organisation the prime consideration may be to keep its highly educated professional workforce up-to-date with technological developments. This is going to support the argument for shifts from synchronous to asynchronous, from courses to resources, from top-down to bottom-up and from face-to-face to online.

For another organisation, say a retailer, a critical determinant of success may be the way they interact with their customers. In this case, the shifts away from traditional approaches will still be relevant, but are likely to be more measured, with a continuing reliance on face-to-face learning.

Learners

The second major way in which organisations differ is in the characteristics of their employees. Each of the following is going to have an impact on which sliders you push, how far and how fast:

- Their prior knowledge. Novices require a great deal of support and structure. Those with more expertise and experience can be more self-reliant.

- Their motivation to learn.

- Their hopes and fears.

- Their confidence in using new technologies.

- Their expectations in terms of how learning takes place at work.

- Their independence as learners.

- The discretion they have over how they allocate their time.

- How long they tend to stay in the job.

Logistics

All decisions are made within the context of constraints and opportunities. Any of the following could make an important difference to your l&d strategy:

- The attitudes and opinions of senior managers.

- The availability of funds to support learning.

- The speed with which the organisation must respond to change.

- The availability of the necessary hardware, software and bandwidth.

- The size of the organisation.

- The geographic dispersion of employees.

Again, you will undoubtedly be able to add to this list.

Preparation is vital

Without a clear and detailed knowledge of the three Ls, it will be difficult to come up with a strategy for transforming l&d that will really work. If you are unprepared and ill-informed, there is a danger your efforts at change will be rejected as inappropriate or ahead of their time. If you tailor your transformation strategy to the needs of your organisation, you could find you are pushing against an open door.

Learning architecture and infrastructure

The 'three Ls' inform and shape our transformation process, starting with the overall learning architecture and the creation of a supportive infrastructure:

Learning architecture

We are all learning machines, constantly adapting to the ever-changing threats and opportunities with which we are confronted. We learn through experience, whether consciously or unconsciously; we learn by seeking out the knowledge and skills we need to carry out our day-to-day tasks; we learn by sharing experiences and best practice with our colleagues, and by taking advantage of opportunities for development, both formal and informal.

The learning architect designs environments that enable specific populations to take maximum advantage of all these opportunities for learning. To do this they need to understand the unique characteristics of their clients and the business challenges those clients are facing; they need to find just the right balance between top-down and bottom-up learning initiatives, between the formal and informal.

A learning architecture provides a blueprint for a working environment that supports and encourages learning. Just like the plans for a building, it looks to the long term, providing strength and stability while also providing plenty of scope for adaptation as needs change.

Learning infrastructure

An architect's plans go well beyond a specification for
materials and dimensions; they also have to take account
of the systems that need to be in place for the building
to fulfil its purpose – the electrics, plumbing, lighting,
security and so on. Similarly a learning architecture
is just the starting point. To function properly,
careful thought needs to be given to the supporting
infrastructure:

- The computing devices available to employees,
  whether desktop, laptop or handheld.

- The networks linking these devices.

- The tools provided to support communication and
  collaboration, including intranets and extranets, social
  networks, email, instant messaging, web conferencing
  systems, forums, blogs and wikis.

- Tools to support the orderly management of
  documents and other forms of digital content.

- Tools that allow for quick access to information on-
  demand.

- Tools to track learning, both for management
  information and to satisfy the requirements of
  regulators.

- Tools, equipment and facilities for creating digital
  learning content.

Thought must also be given to the governance of
organisational learning, bringing together learning
professionals, senior managers and representative
learners to review and approve strategic plans and to
monitor progress. And implementing this strategy is
likely to demand a rethink of the way in which l&d
responsibilities are organised and distributed throughout
the organisation.

Analysis and design

Architecture and infrastructure form the inner layers of our transformation wheel. We need to build on these by establishing new policies for performance needs analysis and the design of solutions.

Performance needs analysis

An effective needs analysis process identifies gaps in performance that can be realistically addressed by learning interventions. It aligns these interventions with business needs and ensures that the right people are trained at the right time, in the right way and to the right extent.

That's the theory. In practice a lot can go wrong, for example:

- You fail to understand the underlying performance issue, making it harder to establish goals or evaluate results.

- You jump to the conclusion that training is the right solution, when in practice there is no underlying problem of knowledge, skill or attitude.

- You misunderstand the nature of the learning requirement and, as a result, make inappropriate design decisions.

- You fail to clarify the exact nature and composition of the audience, with the risk that the wrong people are targeted and efforts misplaced.

- You don't get a handle on the logistical constraints, with the danger that your solution fails to meet your client's needs.

You can't design a learning solution without a thorough performance needs analysis and this takes time, care and good consulting skills. Your starting point should be a clearly documented process that ensures all the right questions get answered.

The design of solutions

It's hard to achieve the outcomes and the efficiencies you require using a single learning method or medium. Today's most powerful and scalable solutions employ a careful mix of learning strategies, social contexts (learning alone, one-to-one or in a group), communication modes and delivery channels. Making choices that satisfy the three Ls (the learning, the learner and the logistics) for the particular situation requires skill and balance.

We may consider ourselves lucky to have so many new choices in terms of learning technologies, and so many ways of combining these with traditional approaches. Unfortunately, what tends to happen is that, when we're faced with a huge range of options, we revert to the old familiar solutions. In other words, we carry on doing what we've always done. If we're more adventurous there's another danger – that we follow the trends and look for ways to innovate at all costs. We have a bundle of solutions and we're desperate to find problems to match.

Again, the answer is a simple and logical process for making decisions on learning methods and media; one that looks first and foremost to meet the client's performance objectives, but which also delivers in terms of the efficiencies all organisations are demanding.

Building 21st century learning skills

The final stage in the transformation process – and outer layer of the transformation wheel below – is the development of the new skills required of the 21st century learning professional:

Thirty years ago, when a new teacher or trainer entered the profession, they would have had a relatively easy task to familiarise themselves with the learning media then available: flip charts, whiteboards, overhead projectors, perhaps an early VHS player. It was achievable to learn how to use all these media, so everyone did. As the years have gone by, the pace of change has accelerated

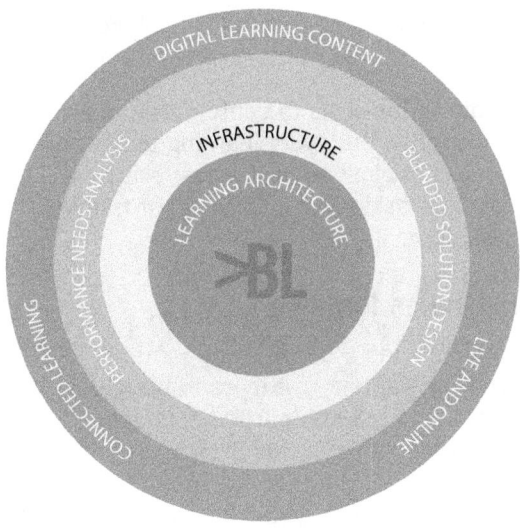

until now it seems that every year there is a slew of new technologies fighting for our attention.

Quite simply, there's now a major skills gap with many learning professionals inadequately equipped to use the latest tools of their trade. This may be because they have not been provided with adequate opportunities to acquire the necessary skills; in some cases they may have simply been burying their heads in the sand.

Creating digital learning content

Digital learning content takes a wide variety of forms, including tutorials, scenarios, podcasts, screencasts, videos, games, slide shows, quizzes and reference materials. In fact we are fast approaching a point at which all learning content will be digital and online.

The skills of digital learning content design are relevant to anyone with an interest in helping others to learn, whether that's a teacher, trainer, lecturer or coach, a subject expert with knowledge they want to share, or an experienced practitioner who wants to pass on their tips.

Some will dedicate themselves to content design as their full-time speciality, but every learning professional should know the basics, just as in the past everyone would have been able to deliver a half-decent training session in a classroom.

Delivering live online learning

Virtual classrooms provide a fantastic opportunity for any organisation that wants to get more training done more cheaply, particularly when participants are widely dispersed. Many of the skills of the classroom trainer can be transferred without difficulty to an online setting, but the experience can still be strange and sometimes a little daunting for those starting off as virtual classroom facilitators. Although formal training can be helpful, the main emphasis should probably be placed on lots of practice with the help of a good coach.

Facilitating connected learning

Since the advent of social media, hundreds of millions of people have been able to build and sustain their personal networks online. The emergence of smart phones and tablets has accelerated this trend by allowing us to stay connected wherever we are and at any time of day. Unsurprisingly, there is a keen interest in bringing these advantages to the world of work, with obvious benefits in terms of learning and performance support.

Connected learning takes advantage of online networks and simple collaborative tools such as forums, wikis, blogs and social networks. It has its place in formal learning, within new blends that extend well beyond the classroom. But its major benefits will occur informally, as a means for on-going support and collaboration.

In some cases, learning professionals can just sit back and allow connected learning to occur naturally on a peer-to-peer basis, but there are situations where their skills in facilitation and coaching could prove really valuable. And novices will appreciate their help as 'curators' who identify useful resources and put people in touch with others who can help them. But before they can do this, learning professionals must themselves become connected.

IN SUMMARY

In this short book, we have described how a transformation can take place in workplace learning and development.

We have set out a vision for workplace learning and development that is:

- aligned
- economical
- scalable
- flexible
- engaging
- and powerful

We moved on to look at some of the changes you could consider making in order to realise this vision, expressed as six shifts:

- from generic to tailored
- from synchronous to asynchronous
- from compliance to competence
- from top-down to bottom-up
- from courses to resources
- from face-to-face to online

And in the final section, we focused on the practical steps you need to take if you are to bring about this transformation:

- Recognising the uniqueness of your particular organisation in terms of its performance requirements, the characteristics of its people and the constraints that govern its decision-making.

- Establishing a learning architecture and infrastructure that recognises these unique characteristics.

- Putting in place processes for improved performance needs analysis and learning solution design.

- Building capability in areas such as the design of digital learning content, learning live and online, and connected online learning.

We hope you have found these ideas interesting and, above all, useful in your work. If you have achieved success in putting them into practice, we'd love to hear about it; and if you need any help, we'd be only too pleased to oblige.

www.ingramcontent.com/pod-product-compliance
Lightning Source LLC
Chambersburg PA
CBHW072248170526
45158CB00003BA/1035